I Come To You
From The Future
Everything You Need
to Know Before You
Know it

John Heffron & Topher Morrison

Happy Af Cheers!

Acknowledgements

John: I would like to thank my wife, who had to deal with me saying "Ugh. I should be working on my book." for a year. Of course my family, and everyone who as ever come to see my shows over the last 20 something years. Also a quick shout-out to my younger self - all your mistakes were perfect and put US exactly where WE needed to be.

Topher: I would like to thank John's wife as well. For several reasons. #1 I don't have a wife. #2 She intimidates me and I don't want to give her any reasons to punch me. #3 If she hadn't been riding John's ass like a donkey to get this done, he wouldn't have been constantly calling me to contribute. I'd also like to thank my parents. It's amazing how the older I become the more I appreciate their wisdom.

Contents

Introduction

During the late 90's there was a song on the radio called "always wear sunscreen" by Baz Lurhmann. It was kind of a trancy spoken-word type song. It originated from a commencement speech Mary Schmich gave to a graduating high school class.

At the time I didn't think much of the song, but for some reason a few of its lines have guided my life.

The real troubles in your life are apt to be things that never crossed your worried mind; the kind that blindside you at 4pm on some idle Tuesday. Understand that friends come and go, but for the precious few you should hold on.

When I heard this song I wasn't looking for advice, why

would I, I was in my 20's. I didn't need any answers. I hadn't screwed anything up yet that I cared enough about to fix.

Now, what feels like a millions years later, I've learned a few things each of which made my life a little better; many of them guided by that lyric from Baz Luhmann's song. My biggest hope is you find one sentence in this book that pushes your life in a similarly positive direction.

That's what this book is all about. Giving you the most important insight and tools you never knew you needed. The 2.5% of stuff that actually matters, that will net you the results you really want in life, whether you know it yet or not. It's not a comprehensive, uber-philosophical treatise on becoming a superior 21st century man. The self-help gurus have that covered, I think. So if that's what you're looking for, feel free to move along and keep shopping.

I Come to You from the Future is all about fast and furious and sometimes funny strategic tips from guys who have been there and done that more times than you can count. My goal is to prepare you to meet your future; so the guy staring back at you in the mirror in 20 years isn't some middle-aged asshole who you want to punch in the dick.

In my stand-up act, I like to joke that at age 25, you're at a pretty magical time in your life. The world is yours. You actually believe that you are going to make it. You probably believe that you know everything. The punchline to that little joke, obviously, is that there is literally no one less equipped to take over the world than a 25 year old who thinks he's got it all figured out.

Of course most 25 year olds don't want to hear or know or recognize this. Not that I blame you, really. There's a reason they say, "ignorance is bliss." Who doesn't want to feel invincible? Still, there have been a few other 25 years olds to come before you. Which means there are people out there who are older than you who might have some experience you could learn from. And if you listened to them, even a little, you'd be much happier when you get to be 30, 40, 50 years old.

Because I promise you: One day the condoms in your pocket will turn into a packet of Tums, and you'll be overly glad you have them when you feel like you're going to die of heartburn from eating a cheeseburger that you forgot to say "hold the onions" on.

Indigestion issues aside, the goal of this book is to share what I have found to enhance my life and what I have done to screw it up along the way, so you can...well, at least have something to keep you entertained while you're unavoidably detained in the bathroom, and perhaps even walk away with a nugget of wisdom to pass along to someone else who could use a little advice.

John Heffron
Hollywood, CA
July, 2013

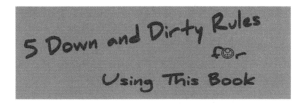

1. Think of this book as a buffet. There's a lot, and it's delicious, but you don't need to eat it all. At least not all at once.

2. You don't have to read this book from start to finish. In fact, you probably shouldn't. You should skip around, a little from here, a little from there (just like a buffet: you don't need the roast beef, chicken and salmon on the same plate).

3. Find a topic that grabs your attention and dive in.

4. Go back for seconds or thirds if you have the appetite.

5. Be skeptical. Just because I found something useful and interesting, doesn't mean you or anyone you know will, so use or share at your own risk.

And that's it. *The rest is up to you.*

All About
You

One Day You'll Realize that Your Bathroom Rug was Never Meant to Get Wet...

...and you'll realize that we just saved your life.

One day you will be out with your girl at IKEA or Bed Bath & Beyond and she is going to buy a rug that looks like someone shaved an English sheepdog and dyed it with an Easter egg coloring kit. The rug, like the purchase itself, will be innocuous—small and inexpensive—to the point that you don't even remember she bought it. This rug will go in your bathroom next to your bathtub and shower.

What we're about to tell you is going to save your life: This rug--the one that goes right next to the tub--is never supposed to get wet. It is decoration. Like your girl's hair at a pool party.

Do you hear that? You stand in that shower until you are completely dry. I don't care if you are late for work or church or your insulin injection. Those towels and rugs are not for you. They are for your wife's imaginary friends who will never, as long as you are married, come over to shower.

Give this to your wife. Let her have it. Those towels and that rug, they are like loom-woven finger cuffs: the more you fight it the worse it gets. Besides, it's to your advantage to let her have this. Because when her imaginary friends do come over, this is what they are going to judge her by. Perfectly folded towels and a clean dry bathmat tell your wife's friends that she has her shit together. A bathroom in disarray means her life is in disarray, which they will both blame on you.

So for the love of god, stay off the bathroom rug. You'll thank me later.

One Day You Won't Know What to Do With Your Life..

...and you'll need to figure it out fast before it becomes your excuse for failure.

Imagine you're headed to this great bar at the intersection of Hot Chicks Street and Free Beer Avenue. You're going along just fine when a big accident blocks the main road. There isn't much you can do about it, so you take a detour that adds several miles to your trip. Then a huge meteor hits the road you used to go around the accident. Now you have to find another detour to get around that giant smoldering hole in the ground. And just when you thought it couldn't possibly get any worse, you see your super confrontational ex at a stoplight. You crank the wheel and hammer the accelerator down yet another road until finally you arrive.

Sounds like a tough trip, right? All these detours and wasted time and energy. It would have been nicer if you could have done it in a straight shot, wouldn't it? Welcome to life. But guess what, you still made it.

Why?

Because you knew where you were going. You had a plan, a destination. Sure, you had to make some adjustments and for a time it may have looked like you weren't going to get there or it was going to take forever.

But you made it.

I meet people all the time who ask, "What should I do with my life?" Most of the time they're not actually asking me, they're asking themselves out loud. At 35 years old, the answer to that question is called a "pivot" or a "career change." At 45 years old, it's called a divorce and a mid-life crisis.

Want to know how to avoid the "What should I do with my life" question when you're 35 or 45 years old? Figure out what you want to do with your life when you're 25 years old.

It's amazing how much time people will spend on anything other than making a plan for themselves. they will waste countless amounts of time and energy on busywork and meaningless bullshit just to avoid sitting down to make a plan. But here's the truth. If they watch more than 1 reality show per week, they have the time to make the plan. Unfortunately, they're just more committed to avoiding their life than designing it.

Maybe it seems like too much work or too much stress to them. Know what's more stressful than making a plan? Failing, because you had no plan. Plus, let's be honest, people who studied and did their homework generally did pretty well. Sure, maybe they didn't take over the world like some of those genius "slackers" who dropped out of school, but those guys are the exception. I'm guessing, if you're reading this book, you don't have the blueprint for cold fusion folded up under your bong like a coaster. You're not the exception. And that's totally fine. Because doing pretty well feels pretty good, trust me.

Seriously, invest a few minutes and make a plan. Write it down!

I will admit that every book I have ever read said "Write something down" and I never have, because that's always been a bit too "Hello Kitty Journal" for me. But you don't need a cute journal or a spreadsheet or a blog. You don't even need to wait for January 1.

You just need to know what your goals are—where you want to go. The smart people with patience create their plan by reverse engineering. They work backward from where they want to go to where they are now. The smart people with no patience just chart a course for where they want to go and hit the gas.

Either way works. It's that easy and that simple and you can start today.

I still don't like to write stuff down, but I do take the time and I do plan. Without it, how else would I know my way around a multi-car accident and a meteor strike and a horrible ex-girlfriend on the path to the greatest bar on earth at the intersection of Hot Chicks Avenue and Free Beer Street?

Do yourself a favor; give yourself a bit of direction.

One Day You Will Discover the Different Levels of Life...

...and you'll avoid becoming a bitter, selfish, and lonely old prick.

Do you ever wonder how similar people can have completely different reactions to the same movie? Or the same food? Or how you can love someone with a deep burning passion, but your best friend (who is pretty much just like you) can hate that same person with the first of a thousand suns?

It's the result of people existing on different levels of life.

Different levels of life? Yes, not so unlike different levels of a video game or a house, we experience life on different levels based on all our previous experiences.

Our experiences have brought us through some weird, stressful, creepy, annoying and interesting things. The older we get, the more of these experiences we've had. If you believe, like I do, that as people we are the sum total of our actions, it goes without saying that all this mayhem has to shape us somehow. You don't fall in love with a girl who your best friend hates without the whole experience changing you. It at least changes the dynamic of Football Sunday, and that alone should be enough to make you pay attention.

There are 3 important levels that can determine your standing in life:

Level 1: The Level of Perception

You simply don't see the world the way it really is. You see the world through a cloudy filter composed of all the stupid, insane things you have seen and done. Your reaction to everything around you is largely determined by the (lack of) transparency of this filter. The more opaque it is, the more trouble you have comprehending there is a world that exists outside your own personal experience. Everything that you see or experience is somehow within you at this level.

Most of Los Angeles lives at this level. I saw it clear as a bell during the 2008 and 2012 presidential elections. Politics aside, it's fair to say that pretty much everyone in L.A. was riding the Obama train. Even little kids and the apolitical types were rocking "Yes We Can" signs, "Hope and Change" t-shirts, "Forward" bumper stickers, you name it. As election season built to a head, so did the excitement.

But then, because the city is a giant bubble where perception dominates, when election night rolled around each time, people were flabbergasted that Obama didn't win by a million percent. How could McCain, then Romney, get as many votes as they did across the country, let alone in their own state??? They were incredulous. These people could not conceive of the notion that anyone would vote for a Republican because, inside the LA bubble, they had never met one.

As a touring stand-up comic, I'd met many. I'd performed for thousands. My filter was much clearer than my friends living inside the L.A. bubble, living at the level of Perception. Which is why I'm writing this book and they're not.

Level 2: The Level of Spirit

All religions preach about the connectedness of humanity. That might sound like some cheesy, ineffectual greeting card nonsense, but there is some truth to the fact that deep down we are all similar. We are brothers from another mother; sisters from another mister. Don't believe me? We share 99% of our DNA. And we all love inter-species baby animal videos. The defense rests.

In reality, the only divisions between us are the ones we make up—Sunni vs. Shia, Red Sox vs. Yankees, Team Edward vs. Team Jacob. Some people will say that these are the things that give us our identity or make us unique. Those people are stupid and haven't had an original thought in their lives. You shouldn't listen to them.

The fact is, you need to drop these artificial divisions if you want to avoid being an angry, lonely old man when you grow up. Instead, focus on the things we have in common at the level of our humanity. That is the spirit I'm talking about. If you can get there, you'll be a leg up on most of the people…especially in L.A.

Level 3: The Level of Responsibility

If we are all connected, then we inevitably have a responsibility to one another, a responsibility to all the people we encounter, to the things we use and to the places we see. After all, every human conflict has one thing in common —two sides. If there is only one side, then there can't be a disagreement unless you're a schizophrenic with multiple personality disorder.

If you can just take some responsibility for your actions, as well as be mindful of the actions and emotional states of those around you, then you will inevitably take a step towards being less of an ass and more of the guy you want to be in the long run.

Which level are you at now? Where do you want to be in the future? If those two questions are making your brain hurt, move on and lighten up. There's more to the future.

One Day You Will Need to Get off Your Butt and Get Stuff Done...

...and you'll be mystified by how exactly to go about it.

Are you a little lazy or a lot lazy? If you're not sure, I've developed a foolproof formula to figure it out:

Count up the number of hours per week you watch TV. Add the number of hours you play video games, then divide the total by your height and multiply the new number by your weight.

If you gave up before you finished that sentence, you're probably pretty lazy. When you're 22 and you have an easy job without a lot of responsibilities, it's ok to be lazy. But that won't last forever and you won't want it to either.

The problem is that being lazy is easy. It's not hard to do nothing. In science, this is called the law of inertia. It's Isaac Newton's First Law of Motion. An object at rest stays at rest, an objection in motion stays in motion. This is a pretty powerful concept that applies to life as much as it does to physics. People who don't do shit, never do shit. People who do shit, always do shit.

That is not the full reading of Newton's First Law of Motion, however. There is a bit at the end that always seems to get lopped off, and is maybe the most important part for young people in your position.

An object at rest stays at rest and an object in motion stays in motion (with the same speed and in the same direction) unless acted upon by an unbalanced force.

What does that mean? It means you'll keep doing what you've always been doing until someone or something kicks you in the ass to either get moving or change course. It means you might need to set a goal (or two or three) for yourself if you ever want to be an effective member of society. It can be a career goal (get a job) or a financial goal (save money to buy a house) or a personal goal (get to the gym). It doesn't matter. All that matters is that you set a goal to, in the words of Motley Crüe, kickstart your heart.

Inescapable Truth: People who set goals simply get more done and do better than people who do not set goals. Objects in motion stay in motion. Objects at rest, stay at rest.

Here is a pretty easy goal-setting task:

Step 1:

Make a list of all of your life goals.

Step 2:

Write each goal on its own 3" x 5" card. Do this with all of your goals, even the most uninteresting or unimportant ones. Just write them all on cards, one goal per card. If you don't have index cards, make them up. Use sticky notes. Just do something.

Step 3:

Every day, pick one of the cards and do something that gets you closer to achieving that goal.

It can be really big or really small, that's up to you. It just has to be something that you actually do (thinking about it doesn't count). Then put that card at the bottom of the pile.

Step 4:

Do the same thing the next day with a different card.

Follow this process every day until you can actually get rid of a card or two because you've accomplished those specific goals (and then maybe add something else to the pile).

This might sound silly and simplistic, but you will be shocked by the kind of benefits you will reap from the act of laying out your goals so you can see them and incrementally work on them. Not only will you make real progress, you'll get there a heck of a lot faster than the losers who talk and talk and talk about their goals but never actually do anything to achieve them.

It's Nike's "just do it" for lazy guys.

Most importantly, this practice will prepare you for when life smacks you in the face (and don't kid yourself, it will). Whether it is some daunting task like being the executor of your parents' estate or an unexpected dose of responsibility like a promotion at work, you'll be ready to get off your butt, shift gears, and get moving.

Just remember: an object at rest stays at rest, an object in motion stays in motion. And you want to be a mover.

One Day You'll Wish You Could Still Visit Your Parents...

...and they won't be around to visit. So spend money on experiences not stuff.

If your parents drive you crazy now and you wish they would just go away for awhile, the day will come that you wish they were around more often to drive you even crazier. Because no matter how crazy they are, you only get one set of parents, and when they're gone, you don't get another...

My dad worked nights for UPS. When we were kids, he'd leave just after we went to bed and get home just as we were waking up. In the fall and winter, as we ate breakfast and got ready for school, he'd tell us loudly (and regularly) to shut the hell up.

I still have nightmares about waking up my dad: He'd charge down the hall in his tighty-whities, with his brown UPS socks still on, screaming bloody murder, threatening to take away any and everything we cared about (TV, allowance, comic books, etc). You'd think I'd be a quieter guy after so many years of this. Oh well.

To this day though, if I see a UPS guy, my first thought is "Everybody be quiet."

In the summer, my dad didn't yell as much. He just kicked us out of the house and latched the screen door behind him. You could always tell the homes where kids got latched out of their houses because the top part of their screen doors would be pushed in by kids pressing their heads up against it to look inside.

We would go out and play for 12 hours. Every day. For months at a time. I would come home at night and my dad would ask, "Are you in for the night?"

"No. Just getting a flashlight. We found some pretty cool guys that live by the railroad tracks. We are going to hang out with them a little bit more."

"Okay, nice to see you."

"Nice to see you too."

Then I would disappear again until it was time to come in for dinner or bed. It's funny but I didn't realize until I was in my 40s that the freest I would ever be to roam the earth was when I was 10. And I owe that primarily to my parents.

Sure we complained about them a ton and they did drive us crazy and embarrass us, but our parents also fed us and clothed us, they loved us and looked out for us, and they taught us a few things along the way (including what not to do).

When my mom was dying, there came a point when she only had a few days left to live. She was in hospice care at home in her apartment, where we all assumed she would peacefully pass away. Unfortunately, that's not how it was going to turn out. The hospice nurse told us she had to leave her apartment and come to the Hospice Care Center. She had a reason that made sense but I don't remember what it was, all I remember is the nurse walking outside and then a lot of crying.

Eventually I gathered myself enough to walk my mom out to the car. I buckled her into the front seat and left the door open so she could have some air while I went back inside to get her things. Before I can turn around, she grabs my hand and leans in to tell me something. I think she's going to whisper some pearl of wisdom or tell me that she'll always love me. Instead, she reminds me to lock up.

Of all the things she could have said, nothing could have thrown me more for a loop. Here I am, sitting outside my mom's place, trying to figure out what to bring from the place she'll never return to, to the place she will never come back from. I couldn't move. Nobody teaches you how to handle someone dying, especially someone close to you. You know how people say 'I didn't know what to do" and they never mean it? I'm by myself in this apartment, looking at all my mom's things, and I truly didn't know what to do.

My mom stressed about money her whole adult life. She was always working to pay down a credit card bill or save for a rainy day. But what comfort was that now? She was dying. Save for what? Pay a bill, to whom? That's when it hit me: comfort. Nothing else mattered more, right then and there, than comfort. I grabbed a bag and threw in the two things that I knew would bring her the most comfort: some of her pajamas and a case of root beer. It was simple, and it probably looked weird when we got to the Hospice Care Center, but it was everything.

So just remember: even if they still dress weird and talk weird and ask for weird stuff and make you feel weird, cut your parents a little slack and appreciate the good stuff while you can.

They'll be gone before you know it.

One Day You Will Have to Stop Eating Crap...

...and your body and mind will thank you.

What you put in your mouth affects every part of your life—from your brainpower, to your energy level, to your short- and long-term health, to pretty much everything else in between. It really is true, you are what you eat.

So if you're currently living on McDonald's and beer, you're essentially a giant fart. Give your body and mind a break. Try a a banana for breakfast instead of some kind of sandwich with the word "Extreme" or "Super" in the name. For an afternoon snack, put down the bag of Funyuns and grab a handful of almonds. At dinner, have a glass (not a box) of red wine rather than a few beers.

Start now and start simple to get yourself used to it. You don't want to be one of those 45 year olds with the hard round belly you can play quarters on. You know the guys I'm talking about. They can't walk up a flight of stairs without shortness of breath, they gets the DTs when they see a salad. To them, lime Jell-o is a green vegetable.

It doesn't end with nutrition, however.

I was friends with a former Mr. Olympia and hired him to train me so I could gain more muscle mass in my arms. Not for any particular reason, just that I'm a guy and guys like to have big arms. Curls for the girls, baby!

When we made it out to the gym, the first things he had me do were heavy squats and lunges. Obviously this guy was slow--your typical muscle-bound meathead who didn't hear a word I said. So I repeated, "I'm really committed to focusing on my biceps and triceps to build some arm mass." With a look and a smile, he replied, "Great! Let's do two more sets of squats, two more sets of lunges, and that should be sufficient for today."

"But I want to increase the size of my arms!" I repeated for a third time.

"You know what? You're right. I'm sorry," he said. "Make that three sets of squats and three sets of lunges, then you should be good to go."

This guy was completely reinventing the definition of dimwitted meathead. I would have told him that too, had he not possessed the ability to clobber me unconscious with one punch. I kept pushing him until, finally, he looked at me and said, "I know you want big arms, but here's the thing: You can't shoot a cannon from a canoe."

I immediately had to take back everything I was thinking and saying.

He knew that my arms could never get to the size I wanted them without building a strong physical foundation in my legs first. "The bigger the legs, the bigger the arms," he said. And admittedly, my legs were, shall we say... chickenesque?

That was the day I began to realize everything in the body was not just interconnected but interdependent. Working one muscle group without working the others can result in injury, lead to an overall physical imbalance, and worse, produce elevated levels of douchebaggery.

Most importantly though, working the body also works the mind. Smart people who work out are smarter than smart people who don't work out. Seriously.

So move your body and start fueling it with more good stuff. Your insurance premiums, your knees and your brain will thank us later.

One Day You'll Decide It's Time to Live Guilt Free...

...and you'll immediately fail miserably because guilt doesn't just magically disappear.

One of our Confucius-like friends has a great saying: "An imperfect action will beat out perfect inaction every time."

People are far too concerned with getting things right and not concerned enough with getting things done. They're scared of doing something wrong or incorrect, and it paralyzes them. We all know people like this--the ones who don't want to try anything unless they know they'll be great at it, for fear of failure and embarrassment. The truth is that many of the most successful people in the world are also the world's biggest failures.

Steve Jobs got fired from Apple—his own company—in 1985 before returning in 1996, when Apple bought his new company for nearly half a billion dollars. We know how the rest of that story plays out (minus the dying part, obviously).

Thomas Edison failed at inventing the light bulb more than one thousand times before finding the right design.

Colonel Sanders' first restaurant failed when he was 65 years old. He took his first social security check and went around to restaurants to find a franchisee for his fried chicken recipe. He was rejected more than a thousand times before selling it to a friend in Utah.

The list of stories like this is a mile long. The point is, though, if you can't handle failure, then it is unlikely you will ever be able to handle success, let alone achieve it.

We'll repeat that: If you can't handle failure, then it is unlikely you will ever be able to handle success, let along achieve it.

Huh?

The only way to live guilt free is to stop avoiding failure. Seriously. You're actively avoiding failure all the time. Knock it off.

Tweet that last paragraph to your friends. Trust me, it's deep.

Instead, focus on taking action towards success, towards achieving. Commit to consistent action.

Just do something.

Take all the time and energy you spend avoiding failure and spend it avoiding inaction. Instead of worrying about failure, worry about inaction. Instead of aiming for doing things right, aim for doing things period.

Because it's not failure or lack of success and achievement that are the sources of your guilt. it is this inaction, this not doing things, that is the problem. The most miserable, guilt-ridden comics are not the ones who spend 200 days on the road. They are the ones sitting at home in their shitty North Hollywood apartments waiting for the phone to ring. Don't be that guy.

One Day You'll Discover There are nly Two Ways of Approaching Money...

...and you're probably using the wrong one.

Taking 'getting laid' as a given, there are really only two reasons people want to make lots of money: they either want to be rich or they do not want to be broke.

Heads up: Wanting to make money because you want to be rich produces far better results than wanting to make money to avoid being broke (see Donald Trump or Richard Branson).

No matter what they say, money is not the root of all evil, and there is nothing fun—at all—about being poor.

If your only motivation to make money is to avoid being broke, then you unconsciously have a set amount which you use to define broke. Even worse, you will simply make sure that you always remain above that threshold – no matter how low it is – and will inevitably fail to reach for anything higher or more meaningful.

If you only want to avoid being broke, then when you're not broke, you have no motivation to make more money. I've seen it happen over and over again with guys I grew up with. They had just enough to not have ulcers and anxiety attacks, and that's exactly where they've stayed ever since.

Now, if you want to be rich, you have a general idea of what amount you would consider yourself rich, and you'll maintain your motivation to meet that amount until you do.

Once you reach that number, the motivation simply changes to "I want to stay rich." In some instances, you may even think your initial number was too low because once you got there you certainly didn't feel rich. That's when you add a little more to your "rich" number and increase your motivation as a consequence.

So, when you ask yourself why you want to make money, make sure the answer involves producing great results in your life and reaching lofty goals. Otherwise you're just trying to avoid being a sad broke loser, and that never works. It's like playing prevent defense against life, except you have no idea how much time is left on the clock.

It's not as simple as setting positive goals, however. You also have to feel like you deserve what you get. Lots of broke people have self-esteem issues—they don't think they deserve money or success or fame or love or much else. Of course, there are also plenty of broke people who think very highly of themselves, but the ultimate goal is never to be a jerk with an over-inflated ego, rich OR poor. Those guys are beyond help for the most part.

Ultimately, it's okay to want more money, a great relationship, a great body—and it's okay to believe you deserve all of that. Just try to be nice most of the time and avoid making money the most important thing in the world—though if you do, be sure the goal is to make lots of it, not avoid making too little of it.

One Day You Will Need Some Sort of a Real Job...

...and You Won't Have to Work at One that Sucks Forever.

When you're 22, it's fine to have a crappy job that you endure because it pays the bills. But do you want to be doing that same job when you're 32 or 42?

When you ask people what they do for a living, it's shocking how many of them can't give you a simple explanation. Those are the people who hate their jobs. No matter how they try to explain it, they make their jobs sound like the most boring things ever. They give you some vague description or a weird answer about what they do; to the point that it's hard to imagine it's actually a job. You really do that? For money? What's that position even called?

The thing is, if you're one of the people with one of those jobs, you know someone's gonna ask you this question. So what are you going to say about what you do? And what are you going to do about what you do?

Here's what you can tell people and here's how you can get out of that crap job before you turn 30…

If you asked a comedian what they did for a living and they said "I'm a stand-up comic," most people would think that's a marginally interesting answer. A better one would be "I make people laugh and smile." Does that sound just a little bit corny? Maybe. But you can't deny that it's also a better, more engaging answer.

Even if you've got the lowliest, crappiest job on the earth, there's always a way to find the silver lining. Somehow, some way, your work benefits someone. Instead of saying "I work in the mailroom," say "I get to meet people every day and bring them valuable information and connect them with others."

It won't just sound better, but it will probably make you feel better about your job as well. Because it's actually true. That is precisely what you're doing when you deliver the mail each day.

Here are some other examples:

Pizza Delivery = I get to show up on the doorstep of families day in and day out and bring smiles to their kids' faces while taking away the stress of preparing a meal for the parents.

Stripper = I get to help executives and business people reduce their stress levels every day by having them forget about their troubles and enter a world of make-believe.

Website Designer = I get to be the Oz of the modern

world and create things behind the scenes. When people observe them in their own reality, they wonder, "How on earth did that happen?"

Start thinking about your job in a different light now – no matter how crappy it is. That's the first step.

The next step is to take that positive energy and think about your next job. Unless you're already living the dream as an assistant car wash attendant, line cook, stockbroker or boot camp instructor, think about what you want to do next. You don't have to blog about it or write it down, but you do need some sort of plan.

What's your dream job? How can you get there?

It all goes back to believing you're worth it, to wanting to be rich instead of not wanting to be broke. Despite what your ex or your step-mom says, you are not destined to work at a shitty job you hate forever.

One Day You'll Want More Control over Your own Life...

...Having more control over your life is no easy thing.

That's because being the determining force in your life is all about focusing on cause, not effect. And understanding the cause of things in your life is difficult if you're not paying attention. Unfortunately for those of you who are still oblivious to your surroundings—like most 25 year olds I meet—causation is how things change.

So pay attention.

Most people like to complain about everything around them, the people they have to deal with, the things they have to do. Yet when they have the power to change things, they don't. These people are crazy. They are literally not connected to their reality. There's a reason they say that the definition of insanity is doing the same thing over and over again and expecting a different result.

The irony is that the people who think they have the most control over their lives and the most control of their environment and their family and friends are living an illusion because, in reality, they have no control over their lives. Maybe if they say it long enough and loud enough, it will come true.

You know those people who go around talking about how spiritual they are? Don't you get the feeling that if they were really that spiritual, they wouldn't have to go around telling everyone about it? Same goes for all those people who insist on telling you how happy they are, how unafraid they are, how confident they are. And the same applies to being the ultimate driver of your life.

The only way to actually get more control over your own life is to take more control by completely changing your approach. You have to think of yourself as The Cause of pretty much everything that happens to you.

A simple way to explain this is to always be on both sides of "because."

If you say, "I have to work late tonight because Tom was late for work," then you're not thinking of yourself as "The Cause." You are simply looking at the effect someone else has on your life and attributing the cause to them. Factually that might even be true, but if you succumb to that tendency you are giving up control of your life because there's no way you can control them, right?

But what if you were to say, "I'm working late tonight because I didn't stress to Tom how important punctuality was." Then you are thinking of yourself as The Cause of the situation, or The Cause of the effects you're experiencing.

YOU are on both sides of the word "because."

YOU are putting yourself into it and accepting that you hold some responsibility for the outcomes you experience... which means you have control. And you can only control how you handle things you're responsible for.

Shazam! You have more control over your life simply by changing your approach and your relationship to a couple words.

Living as if you are The Cause of everything you experience manifests itself in another form--in the difference between necessity and choice. "I have to work late because I didn't stress to Tom how important punctuality was" is very similar to "I am going to work late tonight because I didn't stress to Tom how important punctuality was." But there is a subtle and important difference at the very beginning of those statements: "have to work" vs. "going to work."

In the latter example, the implication is that you wanted to work. It was your choice, not necessity like in the first statement. That is the essence of having more control and less to complain about.

The more you describe things as your choice, the more you'll be able to control your life.

People who truly grasp this technique apply the hell out of it. You can spot them immediately. They walk around with this deep sense of power, everyone in the room picks up on it, and they never have to tell anyone how in control they are. Or how happy, or how confident, or how unafraid.

It's instant, obvious and undeniable.

One Day You'll Want to Make Friends with the Fight...

...and it will make the damage more manageable.

I've done Krav Maga for years. It's an intense form of martial arts founded and used by the Israeli Defense Forces that focuses on neutralizing a threat by being simultaneously on the defensive and the offensive. It was a fitting choice for me because growing up I did everything I could to neutralize even the possibility of a threat of a fight.

One day we were going over knife attacks--forearm to forearm stuff that hurts like hell—when the instructor said something that has stuck with me ever since:

"No matter how much you train for this, even if you trained 12 hours a day every day, if someone pulls a knife, it's a shitty day for you. You are probably going to get stabbed or sliced no matter what you do. The key here is to make the damage manageable. With a knife attack or any attack, you will get punched or kicked and when it happens, you have to make friends with the fight!"

Things that pop up in your life that suck shouldn't stop you. They are just another part of your life. If you have a little bit of direction, and even the smallest amount of appetite for the fight, you'll find that dealing with those things that suck isn't really a fight at all. Everything is workable. Everything is manageable. But none of it is unavoidable. None of us are so special that we are immune to having things that suck happen to us.

That being said, I think it's important to find the real pain points in your life and simply not do them.

Think about the things you really hate doing. Think about how much time you spend thinking about how much you hate doing those things, how much it zaps your energy and drags you down. It's suffocating.

What takes up most of your time? What's the one thing you would kill to get rid of so you could spend more time doing something that moves the ball down the field a bit more?

I travel 40-plus weeks a year. I also have two dogs. When I would come back from gigs, I would have a whole week's worth of dog shit to pick up in the backyard. Now you might be thinking, "John, why didn't anyone at your house do it?" "BHAHAHAHAHAHA," I say to you.

Coming home from every trip, the second I landed I didn't think, "Ah, I cheated death again, the plane landed" or "It's so nice to be home." The first thing I thought every time was, "Ah fuck, I have dog shit to pick up."

Because traveling is tiring and picking up dog shit sucks, I'd usually wait until the next day…or the day after…then before you know it I'd be back on the road again thinking, "Crap, now I have 2 weeks of dog shit to pick up when I get home."

Then it hit me: Do I need to pick up the dog shit? OR Does the dog shit need to be picked up? The answer is dog shit needs to be picked up - but not necessarily by me. That's when I went online and found a company that, for $100, comes to my house three times a week, picks up the crap and takes it away. This is worth a billion dollars to me. I don't even think about it anymore. It's like a utility: gas, water, electricity, shit picker-uppers.

It's not like I solved the world's problems with my free time, but to me, it feels like it. Sometimes I'll see the "poop guy" come and I go right back to my video game.

When you find these pain points--laundry, for example— don't judge. Instead, make a list. Then do some research. There is almost certainly a company out there that will do what you need. For laundry, you can hire a housekeeping service; you can drop your clothes off at a Laundromat and get them folded all nice like your mom did. You can do what a guy I know who hates washing and shopping for clothes does: every month he pays some chick to come in with all new gear and takes away his old stuff. And don't think of it as spending money you don't have--you're buying time. Time to make more money or connections or even nap.

Finding these little low-level pain points that you have control of will make a big difference over the long run. Not only will they make life a little easier but they will give you the time and energy to make friends with the fight over the big things.

One Day You'll Discover Your Mind Is Tricking You...

...but it's your conscious mind that's to blame.

Distortion

We never really think about "the unconscious mind," but it's always in action.

For example you can take a word, scramble all the letters, leaving only the first and last letter of each word in place and people can still read it fluently. Why? Not because they're geniuses. Because the brain does not consciously read every letter of every word, instead it unconsciously reads every word as a whole.

"The olny irpoamtnt tihng is taht the frsit and lsat ltteer be in the rhgit pclae."

One of the craziest functions of your unconscious mind is its ability to take things that don't make any sense and organize them in a way that makes total sense. This is called distortion.

Distortions come into play in our everyday lives all the time.

For example, you might walk by someone every day who you know and say "Hi" to, only this morning they don't say Hi. Then you think, "They didn't say Hi, they must be angry with me!" All the while, this person was actually depressed because their spouse asked for a divorce the night before. Your brain tricked you by distorting reality through the lens of your own perception. It happens all the time.

Deletion

The second way your brain tricks you is through something called Deletion.

You are constantly deleting a huge percentage of the information coming into your brain. Here's some proof. If you close your eyes and listen to the sounds around you right now, you'll begin to hear all kinds of things you weren't hearing only a second ago. Your heartbeat, your breathing, traffic, neighbors, animals, fans, all kinds of stuff.

Why didn't you hear it all before? Technically your ears did register the sounds, but hearing is a cognitive function and your brain was busy deleting it before it could register in your memory because the sounds weren't important to what you were just doing.

This is useful when it comes to concentration. But it can also cause problems if you're not consciously aware of the fact that this process is always happening behind the scenes, subconsciously.

In today's society, everybody wants to be filthy rich, but

very few are. One of the reasons most haven't made their millions already is because they are wasting all their time looking for the quick buck, the fast and easy way. All the while, the old, reliable tried-and-true paths to wealth sit idle right in front of them waiting to be used. And that's because your brain is so focused on getting rich that the only thing it hears are hare-brained get-rich-quick schemes while deleting the slower, quieter methods.

If everybody spent as much time on the slow, tried-and-true ways as they do looking for the quick and easy way to make money, a lot more people would be millionaires by now. What is your brain deleting right now? What financial opportunities are you overlooking because they are not quick enough, or loud enough, for you?

They might take a little longer and a little more work, but they are much more reliable.

So many people are looking for the fastest way to lose weight. "Just give me the quick way, the diet pills! Give me the miracle diet! That is all I want," they say, while the tried and true way (ever heard of diet and exercise?) lies right before their eyes.

Do you know what the tried and true way is for what you're trying to accomplish? If you don't, you should spend some time figuring it out before you get to be my age. It will save you thousands of hours, tens of thousands of dollars, and maybe even your life.

Generalization

The third way your brain tricks you is through generalization.

Our minds have the ability to take the most convoluted and complex things and organize them in a way that you can understand them without ever knowing about or seeing them. This ability can have good consequences, as well as bad.

The brain has the ability to quite accurately generalize something we know little about. If you see something with four legs and a flat surface, it is a table; if it has four legs and a flat surface and a back, it is a chair. These generalizations are a function of memory. It would be pretty tough to get around and function properly if you had to re-familiarize yourself with everything you encounter every time you encounter it. You would probably find a chair much more complicated than you do now.

The problem with this, however, is if what we originally learned was incorrect, we tend to carry those generalizations with us and make what feels like an unending stream of ill-informed decisions: about people, about ourselves, about the world, about life. The most common areas in which we make these generalizations are relationships and money.

Have you ever put in a bid or a proposal and the client chose to go with someone else who had a lower bid? When that happened, did you jump to the conclusion that everyone is price-driven? Everyone goes for the cheapest price? That generalization is obviously false, right? If it were true, how would Porsche and Ferrari stay in business? Or even Cadillac.

Wouldn't everyone be driving a Kia?

How often do you jump to conclusions like this? What single event in your past has put you on the path toward making false conclusions about your current situations?

It's only by being conscious of all three ways our brain processes information that we are able to manage and control the types of thoughts that bounce around our minds on a nearly second-to-second basis. So the next time you find yourself in a confusingly difficult situation, ask yourself: what am I deleting, distorting and generalizing?

This is all a little mind-boggling, but it's some pretty amazing stuff.

One Day You Will Realize the "Difficult Path" is Actually a Lot Easier...

...and you'll weep over all the trouble your young dumb-ass could have avoided.

There are two paths that you can take in life: the easy path and the difficult path. Most people have confused the two. They think that the easy path is the easy path when, in fact, the easy path is always the difficult path and the difficult path is actually the easy path.

If that doesn't make sense, you're probably on the wrong path.

The easy path does look, well, easy. There's really no challenge. No drama. No hard stuff. There is just a TV and a remote control. You don't have to do anything. You don't have to worry about family or friends − you don't have to give a thought to your neighbors or what they're going to say or think about you, and it's all pretty easy.

When you look back on your life, however, you will

come to a frighteningly depressing conclusion: you didn't do anything. You made no mark. Had no impact. The last thing you want to do is get to the future and spend all your time regretting the fact that you didn't do anything; wishing you had taken action, seized the moment, not let life pass you by. That's where the easy path leads.

The difficult path is one of struggle and heartache. Sometimes it sucks. Sam and Frodo don't have a fun time destroying the ring, but they accomplish great things, become legends in their own right, and can live happy and fulfilled knowing they "seized the day." This is where you want to be. Not a mythical hobbit who can't reach the top shelf, but rather the king of your own life.

The trick is to stop wasting time fearing the things you might not overcome. Don't fear the difficult. Embrace it. Enjoy it. It's a heck of a lot more fulfilling and ultimately more enjoyable than the easy path. After all, what value is there in doing something everyone else can do?

The easy path is saying "I am not responsible." It is shifting responsibility (and lots of blame) to others. It is never feeling motivated. It is never being driven to accomplish anything, all the while whining about everything -- from the state of your own life to the state of the country, from the state of your family to the state of the world, all the while never realizing that you could probably do something to change those things you're complaining about if you just shut up and got to work. Sounds kind of difficult, doesn't it?

The difficult path is about taking charge of your world. To do that, you need to take responsibility and that is not always a very fun thing to do. If you don't like the government's foreign policy, take action and try to change it. If you don't like the way people around you are treating you, change the people you're around.

When you get knocked down, get back up again. Sometimes it will be difficult, sometimes it will be fun, sometimes it will be crazy.

That's life. You should probably live it.

One Day You Will Look Back At Your Life...

...and realize the path was there the whole time.

So here's the deal: We all want certain things out of life... at least we think we do.

And we all have a path, even if we're unaware of it. The problem is that most of us make decisions every day, without thinking about that path, and just hope for "the best" outcome.

And that's the challenge...we "hope" but we have no real direction or purpose and no real evidence to see if the result of what we did was good, bad, ok or something else. We make a choice and have no frame of reference for the result because we never bothered to think about the outcome we actually wanted.

One of the greatest ways to think about outcomes, especially good ones, is through visualization.

Of course, subconsciously you visualize things every single day. You want to go to the store and somewhere down deep you see yourself hopping in the car, driving down the street and getting to the store. If you didn't, you wouldn't remember your keys, your wallet, directions and all of the other stuff that you need for your little journey.

However, when you picture the actual outcomes that you want in your mind, it makes major decisions easier and more effective.

Some people freak out a little over the concept of visualizing. With all the controversy around things like "The Secret"—which is all about visualization--they feel like if they tell people they practice visualization, they'll come off sounding crazy or weird. So here's the cool thing about that...you don't have to tell anyone about it. In fact, you shouldn't, because its not about them, it's about YOU. Plus, this way you don't have to worry about anyone's reaction.

The other major challenge with visualization is self-doubt. A lot of people feel like they can't do it. That it's too hard or only smart people can do it. Here's the trick to that: Know yourself. Know how you process information. Some people can picture things, no problem, but others don't think in pictures, they think in words and others in feelings. It's all cool. It doesn't matter how or what you visualize, just that you do it.

By visualizing the outcome of your decisions in some way, it gives you an internal roadmap to follow. It puts you in the driver seat and makes you the determining factor in the outcomes from choices you make..

Here's one thing that visualization won't do contrary to

popular self-help gurus. I should know, I'm a recovering motivational speaker and I talked their bullshit for many years. Visualization WILL NOT make you confident that you can do what you set out to do. And you know what? It shouldn't. Confidence should never come before completion. Confidence happens after you have succeeded and prepares you for doing what you set out to do a second time even better. Look at that 16 year old who is a confident in driving.. they usually crash within the 1st year. It's the cautious 16 year old who drives much safer and is much more aware. If you've never done something before, you shouldn't be very confident. But that doesn't mean you shouldn't give it your best shot anyway.

So often, people are stuck with the consequences of events because they "just happen." Here's the thing: you can either let things happen or make things happen. The moment you visualize an outcome and decide to determine the direction of your future, you have changed yourself from someone who lets things happen to someone who makes them happen. And that's all the difference in the world.

It's pretty cool.

One Day You Will Get Married...

...and you'll experience a bizarre nostalgia for your everyday life.

This is something that can be hard to accept, but it is inevitable. It is going to happen, my friends, that's the cold hard truth. Your wife is going to move in with you. She'll disguise her mission with cute little sayings like, "we're turning your house into our house," but don't be fooled. She's going to come in like a sexy, smiling Bachelor Terminator and eliminate every last vestige of your former life.

I had to get rid of my recliner. I had to get rid of my paper plates. I had to get rid of my roommate, all on account of my wife! Rob. Man, I miss Rob. If you'd asked, "Hey John, what's your big dream for the future? Who do you want to share your life with?" I definitely wouldn't have blurted out "Rob, man. As long as Rob's around, I don't need a big dream. I want to share my life with Rob."

But Rob and I had the best time-all of the time. Rob never jumped around on the couch, or stuck his toes under my butt because they were cold. He never stole the covers or remembered everything I've ever said in the history of ever. I mean, don't be mistaken - I love my wife. I just miss Rob.

I recently told my wife I want her to tell me what to do 98% of the time. It's just easier. At 25, no one should really be telling you what to do. You should be figuring out that stuff on your own. Trial and error. Enjoy it now. Because at 40, it's definitely another story.

Here is what I learned: Now and then, my wife likes to ask me bullshit questions or what I like to call placebo questions that don't really mean anything in the overall scheme of things. She knows exactly what she wants me to say and will happily manipulate me until I say just what she's looking for.

For example, she might say, "I'm going to the store…do you want to go?"

Just tell me if I'm going to the store. I don't know. Am I going to the store? Do you want me to go to the store? Because by the time we figure this out I could have been there and back. And in less trouble.

And I swear my wife sends me to the grocery store just to kind of bring me down a little bit. She sends me for items that don't exist. There should be just a section called "Shit She Wants" and you can rent a little cubbyhole and shop in the Shit She Wants aisle whenever you're out on a non-scheduled, wife-induced store run.

I just need her to tell me what she wants me to say or do. It would be way easier than trying to find the right answers to these placebo questions. Because I'm too tired to figure them out in time for her to be satisfied with my answers, even if they're the right ones.

Yeah, I love my wife a ton, but I still miss Rob. Who's your Rob? Figure it out, then hold on tight for as long as you can. Because he won't be there forever.

One Day You Will Discover the People around You Shape Your Life...

...and you'll be shocked to realize that when you were choosing your friends, you were also choosing how fat you'll be, how broke you'll be and how satisfied you'll be.

The people you surround yourself with help shape who you are. Younger people don't really want to accept this, but when you arrive here in the future, you'll see that it's true. The better the people you surround yourself with, the better off you will be.

If you can be the dumbest, brokest, most incapable person among your friends. you will be destined for greatness.

If you have a bunch of broke, incapable rejects for roommates, they are only going to drag you down. Does that suck? Sure. Quit whining and get some new roommates. If your friends mooch off you and never return the favor, get new friends. Find some people who bring you up a little in the world, rather than drag you down. Find some smart, successful friends. They will rub off on you.

The self-help industry seems to shove the opposite advice down everyone's throats. They start from the position that you don't have to be the effect of your environment and it doesn't matter how bad your situation might be, you can always turn things around. It sounds really nice, because subconsciously it lets you believe that you don't have to change your circumstances in life in order to create a better life. (new paragraph) Okay, I'll admit that for someone who is a victim and blames all the crap in their life on everyone else that might be useful to help them gain some responsibility... but to think that your environment and your friends don't make an impact on your life is just wrong. It absolutely makes a difference.

Context is everything. The people you hang out with and the environment you live in will have a massive effect on your behavior and your future success in life. Recognizing this does not mean you are a victim of it. It doesn't mean you're not in control. It's just a fact you have to deal with. It actually gives you an edge. The only thing that makes you a victim is not recognizing these effects.

Think about it. You and your buddies can paint letters on your chests and go shirtless to a football game, and it's totally acceptable (mostly). But spell out the groom's name on your chest and go to a wedding...?

We are conditioned to behave certain ways and have certain reactions to certain environments.

If you surround yourself with people who do drugs all the

time and party and that is their modus operandi, soon that is going to be your deal, too. That's how it was for most of you in high school and college, that's how it is in the future too. There is a certain point where the mature thing to do is make a change, do something different.

You need an environment where that is possible.

The truth is, you can always change your environment for the better. If you are gaining too much weight, you can always clean out your fridge, throw out all the crap, and leave the yogurt and bananas. You can always go to the gym after work instead of happy hour and lift something besides a pint glass; sweat a little.

Hang out with people who are always outside doing activities, instead of people who are always inside sitting, eating, watching TV and playing video games. If you make those two changes to your environment, you will get totally different results. You almost can't avoid it.

The people and things around you shape your life. You can't deny it. So find some cool people and hang out with them. Because you don't want to be the 40-year old guy getting kicked out of weddings for spelling the groom's name wrong on your chest.

One Day You Will Need Ninja Listening Skills...

...and then you will come to be known as the Argument Assassin.

This day is probably coming sooner than you think. It could even be tomorrow.

One day, your girl will keep saying the same thing...over and over and over again. She'll keep banging away at the message until you actually listen and receive it.

Think of yourself as a front door. Imagine that each time she repeats herself, you receive a Fed-Ex sticker saying first attempt, second attempt, etc., because in her reality, you still haven't accepted delivery of what she's sending you. And she'll keep sending it (repeating herself), making delivery attempts, over and over. And over and over again until you get it.

When you get in a situation like this (being forced into a conversation you don't want to have where you are repeatedly told things you don't really care about), listen very carefully just one of those times and then repeat back whatever she says to you.

That's it. Just repeat back whatever she says to you. It works like a charm. Trust us, she won't notice that all you're doing is repeating what she says.

Here is an example:

Girl: *"Sara doesn't know how to do her job."*
You: *"It's so ridiculous that Sara doesn't know how to do her job."*
Girl: *"I know! You're totally right."*
You: *"Totally."*

See what you did? You just regurgitated back what she said to you in each exchange. You agreed with her, which allowed her to continue onto some other mundane topic of little importance. Piece of cake.

Here's the wrong way to do this:

Girl: *"Sara doesn't know how to do her job."*
You: *"So? As long as you know how to do you yours, who cares how bad she is at hers?"*
Girl: *"You don't listen and you don't understand me!"*
You: *???*

Here's another wrong way:

Girl: *"Sara doesn't know how to do her job."*
You: *"You should tell your boss."*

You might think you're listening, and you might think you're showing your girl that you care, but if she keeps repeating the same thing over and over, then you aren't listening. She isn't looking for you to solve her problems, she just wants you to commiserate. You would have known that if you had your Ninja Listening Skills. In this scenario, you are not the Argument Assassin, you are the unsuspecting guard who gets his neck snapped before he even knows the castle walls have been breached.

We taught Ninja Listening Skills to a friend so he could use it with his step-daughter at breakfast the next day. In most of his previous conversations with her, he had no idea how to respond to her and they typically ended up in awkward silences or tense exchanges that left him dreading future meals.

But then he learned these excellent new listening skills and here is what happened.

"I hate everyone at school"
You hate everyone at school?
"Yea none of my teachers understand me."
Yea they always think they understand you.

(cue 20 min convo)

I've had whole arguments with my girl where I simply shut up and repeated back whatever she said. In essence, she spent the entire time arguing—then agreeing and making up— with herself. And I kept working, doing what I was doing.

Ninja Listening Skills. Become the Argument Assassin.

One Day the Way You Used to Listen to Music will be Totally outdated...

...and people will make fun of you when you talk about the old days.

Remember the crazy old days of music?

You'd be driving in the car and hear a song that you like and the whole time that song is playing all you're thinking is "Please tell me who sings this. Please tell me who sings this. Just tell me who sings this. And, of course, the sadistic DJ never did." They might say, "Come on, that was a great one, wasn't it?" Ha ha ha. Now you have this song stuck in your head that you want to buy. So you have to go to the mall.

Remember those days? Of course you don't, you were 5. Me, I was 20-ish.

When I was at the mall I would make a pit stop at Chess King or Oaktree or Merry-Go-Round. Get myself some Z Cavariccis. An IOU sweatshirt. Some Drakkar Noir. Then I would go to this weird place full of tapes and CDs called the music store. I'd go up to the counter and, in a last gasp to figure out who sang that song I liked, I'd sing that shit to the guy. Oh, it sucked. You'd let the store clear out. And you'd get up to the counter and say, "Hey, man. I'm looking for a song that is very popular right now-everyone is playing it. Who sings it?"

"I don't know. Do you know how it goes?"

"It's like, uh... nobody is gonna break my stride. Nobody is gonna slow me down, oh no. I've got to keep on..."

And even if they know it, they would just say, "No, I don't know what you are singing. You should maybe keep singing. Hold on. Let me get all the girls that work at Jeans West to come in here."

All these girls with shoulder pads and stirrup pants and big hair would come in to hear this little concert.

"Let me rub you up and down until you say stop..."

You have Google. You remember a lyric, you can type it in and boom, you have all the song info. You have an app on your phone. You just hit a button when you like a song and bam, you own it. You have no idea what a revolution that is and why it, more than almost anything else, explains why 40 year olds hate your guts.

Appreciate how lucky you are. And understand that, in the future, your luck will run out. It might not be about music or messages or information, but there will be something that goes right over your head that all the kids will get like it was baked into their DNA. It's the circle of life. Hakuna Matata motherfucker.

One Day You Will Have to Deal with a Pissed-off Customer Service Person on the Phone...

...and you can change their day, affect their life and even get some free stuff while you're at it.

How many times have you called a customer service line and realized that the person you finally got connected to hates their job, hates their life and is about to hate you?

What do you expect? You're the 7 millionth caller of the day (there's no prize for that) and they're expecting you to start bitching about who knows what type of trivial crap that you could have solved for yourself in the first place if you'd just read the manual or unplugged it and plugged it back in.

Here's a surefire method for getting people's attention so that they actually want to help you out.

Remember, most customer service reps immediately expect you to be pissed off, swearing, taking out all your anger on them because your cable was temporarily cut off or some other first world problem. They carry this notion and this general depression about their job into every call…even yours and even if you're nice.

What you want to do is change their perception of you by saying something like this: "Hey Sarah. I know you've probably had a lot of phone calls all day from people who are angry. But have you ever had one of those phone calls from a customer, who even though they have to file a complaint, is so kind and friendly because they realize that you personally didn't do anything to them, helping you to be more grateful for your job and bringing a smile to your face?"

Here's what's cool… It doesn't matter what they reply because you already have your answer: "Well, I'm that customer for you today."

We have all worked a crappy job that we hated because it was nothing but mundane and boring work (you might even work one of those jobs now).

Imagine what it would be like if someone got your attention like that and momentarily snapped you out of the banality of it all. Wouldn't your job become way more enjoyable, even if only for a few minutes?

Ask the customer service person something crazy, give them a fun fact, see how they're doing or offer a compliment. Just try and break the pattern, not just for them, but for you as well.

You'll probably get your cable turned back on faster and you might make someone else's day (or get some free stuff) in the process.

One Day You Will Need to Win an Argument...

...and you can totally manipulate your way to a victory

Everyone gets into arguments—it can't be helped. If you have an opinion about something, some idiot out there has the opposite one. So you have a choice: you can mosey on through life the way you've always done it, keeping your "I win some and I lose some" attitude, or you can learn some super stealth techniques to forever win like a champ.

Please note: The awesome system only works for real arguments. Do not try this if you are having one of those dumbass fights about something imaginary that no one cares about and whoever is less dumb wins. You know what we are talking about.

Here's what almost nobody knows: when you are arguing with someone, almost always, the other person just wants to be heard. They don't give a crap about what you have to say. As a matter of fact, they're probably not even listening to you. They just want you to hear them.

It's so simple, yet so few people really get this.

So, here's the Super Secret Win Every Time Argument Crusher Script:

"I appreciate (that you feel this way - repeat their words) or

I respect (that you feel this way - repeat their words) or

I agree with you that (repeat their words)."

This will let the other person know that you are listening and that you appreciate, respect or agree with them (in some way).

For example, let's say you're debating with your girlfriend about having a threesome and she is on the side of "It's never gonna happen."

She might say, "We're not going to have a threesome because you're my man and you're the only man in my life and I should be the only woman in your life (blah, blah, blah)."

You can then respond with something like, "I agree that we should be the only people in each other's lives." This will help to build some common ground.

Now that you have common ground established, you can proceed with your argument, but this time in a way that lets her hear you, like this…"I agree that we need to be the most important aspect in one another's lives. And that's why we should have a threesome, because the only way that we're going to know how important we are to one another is to have a contrast in the room of somebody who means less to us and who we can treat like a toy."

In this scenario, what you have to say becomes far more

reasonable. Of course, you may not bat 1.000 (particularly in this situation, believe me I've tried it…many a time), but you will have a way better shot. Plus remember, you don't need to bat 1.000 to be an All-Star--.300 will do it.

Listen, repeat, add and learn to argue better (and win more often).

One Day You Will Get Sick of the Drones...

...and you will need a non-violent way to jolt them out of auto-pilot.

Whenever I fly, I get the same monotonous script from the flight attendant who takes my ticket at the desk.

I have the habit of saying something just to throw her off. I want to see if she will answer the question, or if the hypnotic level of boredom from the mindless process she's forced to repeat all day has dulled her brain to the point that nothing can be shake her.

You see, your brain cannot not answer a question. What's the animal called that has a really long neck?

Did you think of a giraffe? Of course you did. You couldn't help it.

I use this question trick all the time to get people to stop thinking. It turns out it's really pretty easy to jolt someone out of auto-pilot. Here is how I board airplanes before my group number is called when I'm traveling for work:

When I hand the flight attendant ,my boarding pass I always

ask "How long is this flight?" So instead of her thinking "I must board Group One, Group One, Group One," I now have her thinking about a different question, which cracks her out of her drone-like state and makes her much more enjoyable to engage later on when I want lots of free cocktails in coach. Try this trick: it works 98% of the time.

When I go to a fast food restaurant and I don't think they are listening to my order I always ask, "Do you guys have showers?" The answer is obviously "NO"—or at least I hope it is—but their lack of preparedness to answer my basic question forces them to re-engage not just with me but with my order, so I can be sure I got my fries with that.

Most of the time when you are arguing with your girlfriend or wife, you know in her head she is thinking "I'm going to say this and then this and then this and he better not say this because if he does I'm going to say this and this and this and this and this…"

The next time you're in an argument, interrupt her right in the middle of it and ask, "Do you smell popcorn?" Watch what happens. It's kind of amazing.

It's fun to see people's reactions in situations like these. Most of the time I can actually snap the person out of hypnotic boredom long enough to earn a little chuckle. At least I got their attention. And who knows, making them more alert might pay off in the unlikely event of a water landing or an unexpected loss of pressure in your relationship.

The more you practice this, the more you wake up the drones, and turn them back into humans. Even better, when you're busy waking up the drones, you'll discover that it's impossible to be one.

One Day You Will Have Trouble Pissing...

...and there's a good thing there's a pill for worse problems.

If you are in your 20s or early 30s, everything probably works "down there" pretty well. All the plumbing is in order. You can drink a beer, go out and take a piss - and if you think you see a cop, you can just shut it down, throw it back in and you're good. You probably think it will always be like that...well, you're wrong.

In the future, you will have some "Wikileaks:" You will be taking a piss and realize you've shaken it for a ridiculous amount of time. For minutes. There is still piss coming. You will get to a point where you think there is no way that there is any left, and when you throw it back in, voila!, soaked boxers. You will probably be wearing khaki pants that show all the evidence, or jeans that soak it all up.

Really? Piss stains on the pants? Everything wet? Your wife will instantly realize it when she does the laundry too.

And don't think she will waste the opportunity to call you out on it. She will… but when you notice anything on her underwear? Just keep moving. There will come a day when you walk by her underwear and you will think, "Yikes! I hope she's working on getting that cleared up as fast as possible." Trust me, inquiring to her about that mystery substance in the bottom of her panties probably isn't going to speed things along. Go ahead and have your questions, but be a gentleman about it and stay quiet.

That's usually when your wife or girlfriend sees your silhouette through the shower curtain and is like, "Let's make love." And your natural response, which you deliver nonchalantly of course, is something like, "Oh, no, I'm good for a little bit. I'm good. I was thinking we don't kiss enough. I think maybe we should just kiss. I just don't feel we're connected. I feel not connected to you because we don't kiss enough. You know, until I see a doctor and get that clean bill of health and then we're good to go again, but in the meantime, I want to see a note."

It's not just you either. Your dog will have questions too. Sure, his are more like, "are there scones?!!" instead of "Hey what's that stuff in the bottom?" But yeah, just don't ask her about it… some things are better left unsaid.

One Day You Will Realize How Dangerous the World is...

...and how much worse it used to be.

It's a miracle anyone over the age of 40 is still alive. All of our parents should have been arrested for neglect. No bike helmets, cribs full of lead, lots of bacon and very little supervision.

When I was a kid I remember riding on the armrest in the front seat of my grandparents' gray Caprice Classic like it was both the coolest thing in the world and nothing at all out of the ordinary.

I'd think, "This thing kicks ass man. Look: I'm higher than grandpa's compass. Hey, dad, grandpa wants a beer for the ride home."

Nobody had a problem with handing grandpa a beer for the drive. Not a problem in the world. It's not like the wind was going to blow beer all over the place. All the windows were rolled up and everyone was smoking.

Then you'd go to your World War II-era elementary

school and suck in asbestos all day as you learned cursive for no reason whatsoever. A is for apple. B is for banana. C is for carcinoma. Have a great day, kids!

And if you got sick, when you came home your mom would dig a big glass stick full of mercury out of the junk drawer and shove it in your mouth. Suck on this thinly encased dose of mercury poisoning for two straight minutes...AND DON'T MOVE or we'll have to do it all over again.. Then if you're really sick, here's a big bowl of ice cream because nothing helps with mucous like more dairy.

But all in all, my parents and my elementary school teachers did keep me safe. And by that I mean, they kept me safe. They took my safety as their personal responsibility, as an element of being a part of the community. That's why, when I was growing up, the big thing was "don't talk to strangers." They didn't rely on product warnings or instructional videos or the fear of litigation to insulate us like they do this generation.

It was a different time back then when it comes to safety, but fortunately some things never change. To this day, if I see a van my first thought is "That is some stranger danger. I'm not helping that guy find his puppy." And I walk the other way.

One Day You'll Notice obnoxious old People Habits...

...only you'll be calling them no-nonsense reasoning, sound judgments, and excellent ideas.

I'm in my mid-40s. It's weird to be in your mid-40s. No one wants to help out a 40-year old. Forty year olds aren't the target of a lot of support. No one is all that proud of you and no one is really worried about you. You kind of have to fend for yourself.

I remember, as a kid, I would always see my grandpa with the same clothes - the same pants, shirt, jacket - every single day of the week. At the time, I thought that was weird. How boring and unoriginal. Why wear the same thing every day?

Now I think it's pretty much the greatest idea ever. It's a uniform, for life. A life uniform. No need to worry about your clothes, about your outfit. Just throw on your uniform and you're ready for the day.

The older you get, the fewer decisions you want to make.

You want to make life easier. You want to eat at the same restaurants and follow the same routine. Why? Because it's easy for your brain to handle. This way your brain can attend to more important, wise, old person things.

When you start hearing yourself talk about things being a "fuss" or "overly complicated," understand that this is what's happening. You're getting older and wiser, and creating more space in your life that you're in control of to do with as you please. And that's a good thing.

One Day You'll Wonder Why We All See Things Differently...

...and you won't like the answer.

There are about a million different reasons why you are unlike any other person. You can find tons of them right under your nose, without even looking.

It's also easy to come up with a million different reasons why you aren't operating at your best or why you haven't achieved greatness like others.

Coincidence? Nope.

Here's why: Explaining away why you aren't living up to your serious bad-ass potential has the easiest of all the excuses, *"Easy for you, but I'm not like you."*

In fact, the majority of excuses in life are variations of that statement:

That's easy for you to say. You're white, but I'm black.
That's easy for you to say. You're black, but I'm white.
Go on vacation? I'm not like you; I don't have money.
Go where? I'm not like you; I'm overweight.

It's not that simple. You're a man, you wouldn't understand.

It's not that simple. You're a woman, you wouldn't understand.

A lot of the time, people excuse their own mediocrity by setting themselves up as different from those who are successful. They couldn't—or wouldn't—do what others have done because their values are different, they're simpler people, they have actual responsibilities, etc. etc.

Successful people, on the other hand, are able to see how we are all connected.

Rosa Parks sat, so Martin Luther King, Jr. could walk.

Martin Luther King Jr. III walked, so Obama could run.

Barack Obama ran, so our children could fly.

These three individuals told the world that they were not different, but exactly the same. Born with the same rights, capabilities and potential, they faced difficult paths on their way to greatness.

Each was working off the idea that people aren't so different, but are essentially the same. In fact, they built their accomplishments on the back of this connection.

The next time you get angry at someone, try to step out of your comfort zone and into their shoes. Try to remember that your opinion, in the end, is just one of a million different opinions, and if you ever want to do anything with it, you need to understand how all of these opinions are similar, rather than different.

Your inability or unwillingness to do that is, at its core, the reason you're practicing mediocrity. Don't be mediocre. Be exceptional, be truly different, by understanding that we're really all the same. Except for Germans, they're just weird.

One Day You'll Want to Buy Something Nice...

...and you'll realize that you need someone else's money to do it.

Don't mess up your credit. I cannot be any clearer about this. Your credit score will haunt you for years--seven at minimum if you screw it up. It'll affect all aspects of your life: you might not get that job you really want, you might not be able to afford the best car insurance coverage, you might not be able to get the cell phone plan you need.

You don't think about credit when you're in your 20s, I understand that. Credit doesn't have breasts or alcohol inside it, why would you spend any brain cells thinking about it? Just know that by the time you realize that your negligence has destroyed your credit that will be the exact time you want and need credit the most.

When all your friends are buying houses, leasing nice cars, and financing their kids' private school tuition, you'll still be living in that lame apartment, driving that same beat-up

Honda Accord, and walking your daughter to her fenced-in public elementary school during that one week every month you have custody of her. That's what bad credit can do to your prospects over time. And if you manage to actually get a loan when you need it, don't think it won't cost you 50% more in interest than your old buddies with good credit. Banks may be full of greedy criminals but they're not full of idiots.

If you took most of your 20s off from fiscal responsibility, there's no use in kicking yourself or beating yourself up over it. What you need to do instead is right your ship and start chipping away at your debt and your credit score.

If you have to move back in with your parents or live with four roommates to save money, DO IT.

Unless you have absolutely no income at all, DO NOT defer your student loans. When you defer your student loans, interest continues to accrue and that interest is capitalized at the end of every year. That means it gets added to the principal and as your principal goes up so does the balance against which interest accrues. All of a sudden the $20,000 you borrowed to get drunk and hook up with hot girls that one year at college before you dropped out to sell stereo equipment with your cousin has increased to $35,000 and you'll be paying back loans until your old and gray. Pay what you can, trust me it's worth it.

You've got to start doing things like this as soon as you can. Because soon you're going to meet someone you care about and want to provide for and protect. You're going to want nice things, not just for her but for yourself. Those things are going to cost money. Sometimes LOTS of money. And I'm gonna go out on a limb here, but chances are you don't have lots of money.

That means you'll have to rely on other people's money to get those things: banks, friends, family, credit unions, employers. All of those people are going to evaluate you as a credit risk. Some of them, like the banks and the credit unions, will look at the numbers on your credit score. Others, like your friends and family, will look at your busted ass car and your janky old apartment.

You have to give them a reason to trust you with their money. Only then can any of us trust you with something nice.

One Day You Will Realize Some of the Best Advice Doesn't Make Sense until It's Too Late...

...and this is the best one.

If there is one group of people on this earth who could use a little advice it's young people who think they're invincible. And there is one piece of advice they need the most, precisely because they're never in a million years going to listen to it.

We are actually a little hesitant to give you this advice because we don't want to completely burst your bubble. Maybe you are invincible. Every now and then, some naively optimistic person is certain they're capable of anything and actually does something awesome.

Regardless, this is the advice: Don't be afraid to believe you are as invincible as you think you are, but be smart enough to know when you're not.

Huh?

Right now, you have no idea how valuable and important this advice is. You'll get it when you're older and by then it will be useless. That is just the way it is.

One Day You Will Be Baffled By How Someone Who Seems So Reasonable Could Act So Crazy...

...and we are here to solve the mystery.

Ever wonder what makes people do what they do? Do you ever find yourself asking why the heck is that person acting so crazy?

Why does one person get rich and the other goes broke? Why do some people stay loyal and others cheat on the ones they love? What determines who becomes a world-class athlete and who becomes a total couch potato?

Most people might seem a little crazy and unpredictable on the surface, but it's actually pretty easy to figure out how they'll act--it's all about their own values.

Values are like mental maps, the things that give us purpose and drive us. For Donald Trump or Jay-Z, money and success are likely big values, which they've both been able to live up to many times over. If you ever want to know what The Donald or Mr.-Z are going to do in a given situations, you can be sure that money and success are going to be the drivers of their decision making process.

But that information is only valuable to the extent that you are working with them or are affected by the decisions they make. More often than not for most of you, that won't be the case. So before you get preoccupied with figuring out other people's values, you'll want to discover your own values first. That's something you can actually use to your benefit.

These may not be as obvious as you think because most of us don't really know what we believe in or care about. We think we do, because we don't think about it very much and we let other people do the thinking for us. That's why so many people are unhappy, I think. It's only when you figure out your values that you can really know what the right choice is for you, what is best for you, and have confidence in your decisions.

It's when you don't know your values or aren't aware of them enough that you find yourself miserable, kicking yourself, wondering why you made all these stupid decisions that didn't go anywhere..

Some people think that you always get what you value, but this isn't always the case.

This is because you can compartmentalize your entire life into six simple categories:

1. Spirituality
2. Career and finance
3. Personal development
4. Relationships

5.   Health and Fitness

6.   Family

(You might have 6, 8, 12, 20 or 2 categories. It doesn't matter; however you want to set up your life is just fine.)

The older we get, the more we believe that our main areas of life should not be placed in order of importance, but rather given equal amounts of attention and focus.

Anyway, it seems that within each of these categories, we assign levels of value or importance.

For example, one person might value money in their career, while another might value teamwork and fun in their career. These two people would most likely seek out completely different professions. And that's great.

Another person may not value money in their career, but place high value on it in relationships. This person would probably only be attracted to a wealthier spouse but be content with taking a job that doesn't pay a lot. Again, it's all personal and it's all cool.

If we don't take the time to identify what we want and value in life, then we will continue to drift through life on autopilot, with no real purpose. This might be fine when you're 21, but it will definitely get old before you turn 30. When we don't know what our values are, we end up doing things counter-productive to what we want in life.

Look around at your life and see what you've got going for you, because at the unconscious level you almost always get what you value. When you desire something that much, your unconscious mind is always on the lookout for opportunities to fulfill those desires. It will get you up early, keep you up late, increase your motivation and move you a long way in the right direction. The fulfillment of these values, while not effortless because you have to put in the work, is seemingly trouble-free.

In the meantime, most of us are still working with our conscious values. These are the things we tell the world mean everything to us. The more these two sets of values match up for us, the easier life is.

One Day You'll Discover Forgiving and Forgetting Is Hard...

..and if you wait too long, it only gets harder and you might miss your shot.

Let it go.

Just let it go.

That's not just dramatic advice from a goofy meditation guru, it's one of the most valuable things you will figure out in the future that you may not know now—just let it go. Forgive and forget and you will be so much happier.

A lot of us are carrying baggage that is just a bunch of sad sack stories. We use those stories as excuses for why we can't do something, why we haven't achieved. Maybe our dad missed the big baseball game when we were 10, or we don't have enough money or we were born under the unluckiest star in the world. We are in love with our excuses and often cling to them for dear life, like an abusive co-dependent relationship.

It's amazing how a lot of us go through life just looking for that pat on the back that we never get, even though by any other measure we're really successful. You know you've met those crazy insecure guys who are running their lives like they just want a pat on the back from their dad. He's never given them one. And it's really something that would change their whole freakin' life.

You have two choices in this situation: 1) you can do something about it and ask your dad for that pat or, 2) you can let it go and move on. Don't live your whole life waiting for that pat, because unfortunately it's not coming any time soon. And that's if you actually deserve it.

It's just as likely that you're not quite as amazing as you think you are. You should deal with it and then let that go, too. A good place to start is to say you're sorry once in a while. Say it and actually mean it.

But forgiveness…ah, forgiveness, the thing we're really, really terrible at practicing. That's where the real battle is. Usually we're just so self-righteous about it.

It kind of sounds like this: "You know that shitty thing you did to me? I forgive you for that. Don't get me wrong, you messed up and it was totally all your fault, but I'm going to forgive you now."

That's really not forgiving anybody. That's just trying to look superior and act like you're over it, when in fact you're still probably pretty pissed off. If you really want to forgive somebody, you need to realize that it's not about them, you're actually doing it for your own damn good. You can finally get that monkey off your back, so you can breathe deeper and go about your life.

You don't have to make a big drama about it or even say "I forgive you." Just say "thank you."

Then be a man and let it go.

In a Word

One Day You Will Find Yourself at the End of our Book

If you've read this far, you either must be getting some cool learnings, or you are just the kind of person that likes to go to the last chapter and see how shit ends before you decide to buy it. If it's the latter, trust me, you missed some gems... like how to manipulate your girlfriend into thinking you are a great listener, and what to do when your dog goes all buffet on your underwear.

Let's lock all these pearls of wisdom in. I want you to image your future self. Make yourself way old, like 50. See yourself surrounded by the people you love. Imagine standing in front of your dream home with the car you've always wanted parked in the driveway. Are you married? How does she look? Do you have any kids? How many?

Now what if you walked up to the ancient 50 year old you. What would you say to you? (besides asking them why they are wearing such lame clothes.) What if your 50 year old self talked to you and said;

"Hey listen, you are going to have an amazing life. But to get this life - this house, this car, this amazing wife, and these incredible kids there are some things you need to start doing now, and some things you need to stop doing as soon as yesterday."

What would he tell you that you need to start doing? Write those down in your book now...

What would he tell you that you need to stop doing? Write those down in your book now...

Let's save you a ton of cash right now on self-help, therapy, drug addiction, lottery tickets.

Whatever things you wrote in those spaces above, or whatever things you thought about writing but were to lazy to write down because you couldn't reach a pen? That's your answer.

And nobody told you that but you. It wasn't your know-it-all friends; it wasn't your nagging girlfriend; it wasn't your overly-concerned parents. It was you. So stop doing shit that you know you should stop doing, and starting doing the things you need to start doing. Man up and start down the path.

The rest is just you making friends with the fight...

Making it Really, Really Simple

In case you're not much of a reader, we have made this insanely easy for you. Following is our entire book distilled down into a few sentences – read it, weep, enjoy.

- Don't get the bathroom rug wet. Better yet, don't step on it at all.
- Make a plan.
- Figure out what level of life you're at and if that's really where you want to be.
- Don't be so damn lazy.
- Visit your parents.
- Learn to memorize.
- Stop eating so much crap.
- Just do something.
- Stop complaining and blaming and take control of your life.
- Make friends with the fight.
- Ask if your brain is telling you the truth.
- Make things happen, don't let things happen.
- Someday you might get married and miss your old roommate
- Sometimes it's simpler to just let your wife tell you what she wants you to do.

❀ Hang out with people who bring you up instead of drag you down.

❀ Learn to listen and repeat what you hear.

❀ Enjoy the music.

❀ Be nice to customer service people.

❀ Learn to argue better.

❀ Help people escape being drones with a little humor.

❀ Focus on getting rich as opposed to not being broke.

❀ Figure out what you next job might be.

❀ Don't make too much fun of old people because you'll be one sooner than you realize.

❀ The difficult path is actually easier than the easy path.

❀ Wikileaks will take on new meaning to you in a few years.

❀ It's a dangerous world out there—be glad you didn't have to navigate the perils of childhood 40 years ago.

❀ We're all connected somehow.

❀ The best advice now won't make sense until you're older and there's nothing you can do about that.

❀ Figure out what you value in life.

❀ We all have a different way of looking at things. Deal with it.

❀ Forgive and forget.

❀ And wear some sunscreen.

Who We Are and Why You Should Care

(Just a Little)

Who are we and why should you give a damn or listen to anything that we have to say?

Great question.

First of all, we are two guys who survived our 20s and our 30s. That should be enough for some of you guys, because we did and said and thought some really, really stupid things in those 20 years. Beyond that though, we've gotten a little smarter and a little savvier along the way. If we can spare you the loss of a little dignity and stress and give your sanity (not your vanity) a boost along the way, then our work here is done.

JOHN HEFFRON: I'm at a weird in-between stage now in my early 40s. I bought high tops recently and had to ask myself, "Am I too old to wear high tops? Is it weird?" I know I don't want to buy any more sweatshirts advertising fake athletic departments or with a number on them for no reason at all. I'm too old for that, I'm just not sure about the high tops.

But I'm also not old enough for Tommy Bahama. I'm not making fun of Tommy because some time, maybe pretty soon, I will say, "Damn, these shirts are comfortable and stylish," and I will wear them proudly with my visor and low-rise sneakers. Hopefully no fanny pack.

But enough of about my wardrobe: What I'm really saying is that I'm old enough to know better, but not too old to be clueless. I probably have an idea or two (if not a fashion tip) that you can borrow and use to get ahead with. That's why you should listen to me.

TOPHER MORRISON: Pretty much what John said, except for the Tommy Bahama shirts…I'll never wear them no matter how old I get. If you want to know anything more you can google me.

Resources and links

John Heffron:

John Heffron is an awarding winning comedian with numerous comedy specials, TV appearances, and he was also your age once.

https://www.facebook.com/JohnHeffron
Twitter: @johnheffron
Web: http://www.johnheffron.com

John's comedy specials and albums are available on iTunes.

Topher Morrison:

Topher is an author and corporate speaker.

Twitter: @tophermorrison
Facebook: facebook.com/professionalspeaking
Web: http://www.tophermorrison.com

A THANK YOU FROM US

OK so because you believed in us and bought this book, we want to give you crazy gift that's valued at hundreds of dollars. No matter what age you are (if any point you felt this book was written for someone younger then you... here's where it all pays off) this is a pretty sick deal as a thank you from us to you for hanging out with us for a hundred pages or so:

THE MENTAL GAME OF LIFE HOME STUDY COLLECTION
(Available immediately for online viewing)

Like any other game, life has certain rules and maneuvers that will bring about positive results – and a number of pitfalls to be wary of. As well there are understandings and techniques that can make you an ace player. The arrays of equipment we all bring to our lives are our talents, language, intellect and our awesome capacity for achieving. Wouldn't it be great to find out:

- How to effectively play – and the many ways our thoughts can make things happen for us?

- What the best strategies and combinations of moves are to get a desired result?

- How to make your moves from the powerful position of knowing that the game doesn't have to be a Win-Lose scenario – it can be a powerful Win-Win, where you win big!

This seminar addresses the most important element of piloting your life adventure...the mental aspect.

Do you want to experience these results now?

- ✳ Overcome procrastination and fears that have been holding you back
- ✳ Transform from pay check-to-pay check reality with 3 psychological techniques of the millionaire mindset!
- ✳ How forgiveness can open the floodgates of wealth, health and love!
- ✳ Create more CONFIDENCE and ENERGY for your life
- ✳ Rekindle the spark in relationships
- ✳ Successful negotiation with your employer, coworkers and employees
- ✳ Develop and really enjoy a healthy diet/lifestyle
- ✳ Get more accomplishment and joy out of life
- ✳ Effective communication with your kids – and your parents
- ✳ Take action for what you're after... etc.

The Mental Game of Life will give you the tools you need to achieve these results.

Since this is a heck of a deal, we're asking for one small favor - please take just a few minutes to review this book right back where you bought it on amazon.com. The star rating and reviews have a huge impact on other readers' decisions, and your honest feedback is greatly appreciated.

To view The Mental Game of Life for free, just visit:

www.icometoyoufromthefuture.com